# THE STORY OF CINEMA

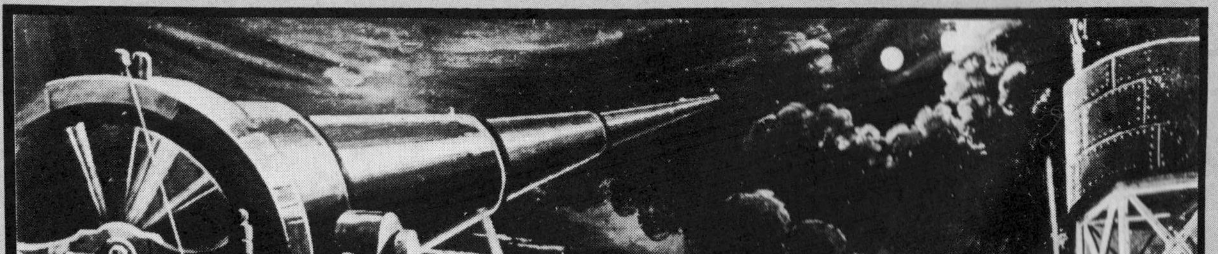